Climbing While Rhyming

Climbing While Rhyming

A Poetic Ascent to the Foot of the Cross

Norm Wymer

No portion of any poem was created by AI (Artificial Intelligence). This is all inspired by the Holy Spirit.

Cover design by Jennifer Lassiter
Editing by Jeff Ferris
Logo design by Lisa Hurley

www.normwymer.com

ISBN: 979-8-9892188-0-6

Dedicated to my incredible family and especially my lovely wife, Kim. She is my Barnabas (encourager), the motivation for me to start writing poetry from the heart, the love of my life and an incredible example of how to lead a Christian life.

Father God, thank you for the ability to write these poems and putting them in my head. May they all glorify You, because that is why You made each and every one of us.

Ephesians 2:10 - For we are God's handiwork, created in Christ Jesus to do good works, which God prepared in advance for us to do.

Endorsements

"The definition of the word poetry is generally defined as 'a form of literature or verse in which special intensity and concentration is given to the expression of important feelings, thoughts, and ideas with the use of distinctive style and rhythm'. In a nutshell, poetry is designed to create a connection that makes the reader think more deeply on a subject that is relevant and important to both the poet and reader. Poetry is designed to help us THINK. To that end, my gifted engineer and business leader friend, Norm Wymer, has created a book of poems that a number of us encouraged him to publish. His poetry has helped many of us in his circle think more deeply about a myriad of important topics such as faith, love, family, obedience, gratitude, caring, prayer, work, reflection, and life in the 21st century. In these times of exceptional busyness, his poetry possesses the power to help us slow down and reflect on some of the truly important lessons and things that make life such a blessing. Thank you, Norm."

Clinton O. Longenecker, PhD.
Distinguish University Professor of Leadership Emeritus
People and Organizational Transformer
Amazon Best-Selling Author

"Norm uses a great mix of poignant prose with clever quips, dry humor, and great insights to draw inspirational reflections about life challenges, our relationships with family, friends and God to help guide us and grow us in our relationship with our Heavenly Father. I love the acrostics and Biblical references that amplify each weekly theme. Norm has covered just about all the 'bases' with a devotional that builds my faith and challenges me to go deeper in my walk with the Lord."

Paul Schweer
Retired President, Financial Express
Treasurer, Westgate Chapel, Toledo, OH

"I enjoy reading these poems. The words in these poems flow out of Norm's heart, as he looks to Christ, while looking at life and life's events."

Gloria Adelphia

"Like David, Norm Wymer is a man after God's own heart. And like David's writings, this book is filled with poetic musings that reflect that heart for the Lord. You will be blessed as you read through and contemplate the beautiful truths within."

Jim Lange
Author of *Calming the Storm Within: How to Find Peace in this Chaotic World*; and *The Happy Wife Happy Life Deception: How to Stop Walking on Eggshells and Be the Man You were Made to Be.*

"When he writes, Norm rolls up his sleeves and reveals his heart. The man, the spirit, and the effort behind this book will bring hope and encouragement to those who engage it and desire to walk with Jesus."

Jeff Ferris
Writer / Editor - Reach In Word, LLC
reachinword.com

"Having met Norm our freshman year in college, I have known him as a true Christian, seeking out Jesus in all that he does and everyone he sees. He is an inspiration to many, truly letting Christ's light shine through him in all ways. He began sharing his poems with many of us several years ago, and I have counted them as one of the blessings in my life. I pray that they too inspire you in your journey towards a greater relationship with Jesus and all of His people."

Mark Thomas, General Motors Institute, 1984
Retired Director, Electrical Engineering – Daimler

How to use this daily devotional

- **Monday** – Read the poem – document any thoughts, Bible verses or feelings, which may spring up.
- **Tuesday through Saturday** – Start with the "Acrostic" word in CAPS that go downwards – the acrostic is one of the key words / focus of the poem. Meditate on how this affects your life, your thinking, your relationship with Jesus.
- **Saturday** – review what you have written earlier in the week. Prepare your heart for the corporate worship you will experience at your church.
- **Sunday** – worship Jesus and contribute to your local church.

I pray this can be a blessing to you. Thank you for purchasing this devotional. I pray it brings joy and a closer relationship with Jesus.

Peace and Joy,

Norm

EXAMPLE

Let's face it, many Christians are afraid to share their faith. We come up with many excuses and the majority of those excuses are based out of fear. What if there was a way to look at sharing our faith through a different lens? What if it has more to do with God's love than our method? Some thoughts for us to ponder....

A part of life which causes most Christians grief
*Is an innate **fear** of sharing their belief*
Of the resurrection and God's saving grace
And how death on a cross saves the human race

Satan is crafty and will plant in our mind
Excuses for not sharing of every kind
But after considerable thought, I must concede
It is God's delight that I plant many a seed

I must stop assuming and taking for granted
That others will sow seeds which have been planted
For my job is to throw seeds all over the ground
To share the gospel message the entire year round

Forget about whether I know chapter and verse
Just show God's love, no need to rehearse
For every seed thrown, has the potential to grow
It's the ultimate act of kindness one can show

Monday: READ THE POEM and write thoughts:

Father God: I admit I have fear when sharing my faith. I don't understand why. Possibly Satan puts it in my mind that I have doubt – I'm not a good enough Christian, etc

EXAMPLE

Tuesday: Fear - 1 Samuel 12:24

I Sam 12:24 – I am ONLY to fear the Lord and serve Him
Why do I worry about what humans think of me? Father God,
please give me grace in this area. Help my boldness.

Wednesday: Evil - Psalm 23:4

Psalm 23:4 – "I will fear no evil" for You are with me

Thursday: All - Psalm 33:8

Psalm 33:8 – Let all the earth fear the Lord; there is no
reason to fear man; God is the only one I should fear

Friday: Reproach - Isaiah 51:7

Is 51:7 – "do not fear the reproach of mere mortals or be
terrified by their insults. Wow! This is powerful. God, thank you
for this fact.

Saturday:

I can share my faith and not worry about what people think of
me. Because I love You and love people, it will be easy for me to
share my faith—it is me being obedient to Your Word. Thanks, God.

Week One

These disciples ran and hid after Jesus was crucified. What gave them their courage in the aftermath? The empty grave. Eleven of the twelve disciples died for their faith in Jesus.

But you, O Lord, are a shield around me
Only to you, Lord, can I make this plea
You are the glory. You are my story
You hold my head high; I'll follow your way
To bless me with your Spirit is what I pray

You lifted up all lives that you crossed
Your life dedicated to saving the lost
All while knowing Your ultimate fate
Of saving those, yes, even those who hate

Sometimes in my life, it's tough to cope
But to anyone who seeks You, You give hope
Only through You, Lord, can I be brave
My courage secured by the ***empty*** *grave*

Monday:

____

____

____

Tuesday: Empty - Ruth 1:21

Wednesday: Mind - 1 Peter 5:8

Thursday: Pray - Matthew 6:9

Friday: Trust - Jeremiah 17:7

Saturday: Youth - 2 Timothy 2:22

Week Two

JD Farag always ends his sermons with the ABC's of the gospel (see the last pages of this book). He uses Romans 10:9-10, which partly states: "and believe in your heart that God raised Him from the dead, you will be saved." It's very simple, my friends.

I discuss with those who have an objection
To a total belief in Jesus' resurrection
A belief which will affect eternal direction
An event which stands up to the most critical inspection

Jesus asked Peter, "Who do you say I am?
The Christ, the Messiah, the God of Abraham?"
They thought Jesus the leader Who would crush and defeat Rome
Not realizing the power of rising from the catacomb

Jesus' death left the disciples very lost and confused
Scared for their lives, all hope and faith diffused
Like defenseless lambs, scared and cowardly
But that all changed at the breakfast next to the Sea of Galilee

So what occurred, making these men unashamed?
Now speaking brazenly, the gospel being proclaimed
What caused these men to suddenly become so brave?
It is simple; Jesus' resurrection from the ***grave***

Monday:

____

____

____

Tuesday: Gather - Leviticus 8:3

Wednesday: Reach - Psalm 144:7

Thursday: Afraid - Matthew 10:28

Friday: Veil - Mark 15:38

Saturday: Endurance - 1 Timothy 6:11

Week Three

Sometimes we battle a lot in our minds, which distract us from focusing on Jesus. Personally, I have been a "habitual worrier" my entire life, which I have maligned into believing this means "it shows I care more." I have come to understand worry and anxiety is of Satan and meant to distract us from our true focus.

Peace cannot co-exist in us with fear or ***worry***
The Bible's very clear on this, not fuzzy or blurry
Peace is a fruit of our great gift, the Holy Spirit
There are teachings to help us, if we have ears to hear it

Worry *is an attack by Satan upon our mind*
Combining worldly concerns which are cleverly designed
To destroy our peace which can never be aligned
If our psyche is of the flesh and grossly maligned

In Matthew 6, we are taught to ***worry*** *about naught*
Our life provided for, we should not be fraught
Do not ***worry*** *trying to figure out tomorrow*
Anxiety is unhealthy and will add to your sorrow

When the enemy attacks, counter with prayer and petition
Yes, parry with the weapon used by our Great Physician
Cast your ***worries*** *upon God, and be less stressed*
Naturally lean on Him to enter into His rest

Monday:

____

____

____

Tuesday: World - 2 Corinthians 10:3

Wednesday: Optimistic - Jeremiah 29:11

Thursday: Reverence - Malachi 2:5

Friday: Redeemer - Ruth 4:6

Saturday: Youth - Proverbs 5:18

Week Four

Matthew 7:26-27 – Building your House on Sand

Based upon a YouVersion™ devotional. I pray you have a solid foundation beneath you in these crazy, wild days. If not, I know where you can find one! Be blessed!

Have you built your house on ***sand****?*
Life hasn't gone exactly as planned
You hold your ground, you take your stand
To find that you don't like your brand

You're thinking it's time to maybe rebuild
No longer happy, you're not so thrilled
The fact is that your spirit has been killed
You're wondering where your heart can be filled

You ponder where you started to stumble?
Where did the grasp slip and the ball fumble?
The foundation is cracking and beginning to crumble
Maybe time to regroup and consider being humble?

Time is ebbing; look carefully at the clock
I pray you consider and closely take stock
Open the door; there is a gentle knock
Build your house on Christ, the Solid Rock

Monday:

Tuesday: Sand – Matthew 7:26

Wednesday: Abraham – Genesis 22:17

Thursday: Numberless – Isaiah 48:19

Friday: Descendants – Genesis 32:12

Saturday: Are there areas of your life where your foundation is weak?

Week Five

- Does the fruit of my life reveal that the Christian life is about me OR about God's purposes for my life?
- Am I stewarding the resources God has entrusted to me in such a way that I can be a part of the work that He has called me to?

We are managers, we do not own
All our possessions are really on loan
From God, we are stewards of His assets
We should manage these gifts so we have no regrets

When the Christian life becomes about "me"
Rather than God receiving all the glory
When I focus on what I get, rather than what I give
It will undermine the true reason to live

What does the fruit of my life reveal?
A tender heart, or one made of steel?
Do I invest my time and talents for a godly reward?
Showing faithfulness always to my Lord

Yes, God has a purpose for me while on earth
For which He's been preparing me from my birth
To live for Him, and maybe write a poem or two
And ***focus*** *on the work that He has called me to do*

Monday:

Tuesday: Friend - John 15:13

Wednesday: Overwhelm - 2 Samuel 22:5

Thurdsay: Children - Proverbs 22:6

Friday: Uncertainty - Hebrews 11:6

Saturday: Sin - 1 John 1:8

Week Six

- Let's ask ourselves the following questions:
- What do we see in Jesus? His compassion grew out of the needs of others, not His own needs.
- What did Jesus see in people? Jesus saw people as they could be in His freedom and He loves us too much to leave us the same.

If we truly want to replicate the heart of our Creator
We must have compassion, for there's no feeling greater
Opening our minds to see through Jesus' eyes
A love for all people we must prioritize

Whether a person be a leper or a centurion
A newborn baby or an octogenarian
Because we emulate Jesus, we cannot exclude
Our Christian love must extend to the multitude

The fearful, spiritually bound, or those with a broken ***heart***
We must sacrifice for those whose world's coming apart
Don't see people as they are, but rather what they can be
Grace freeing them from sin's burden is Christ's solemn decree

The needs of people must trump our own
Help lift their burden, remove from their neck a millstone
We must acquire the actions, the ***heart*** *and the mentality*
Of Him Who gave His life at Calvary

Monday:

Tuesday: Help - Ecclesiastes 4:10

____

____

____

Wednesday: Endure - 1 Chronicles 16:34

____

____

____

Thursday: Anger - Colossians 3:8

____

____

____

Friday: Repent - Job 42:6

____

____

____

Saturday: Thankful - Philippians 4:6

____

____

____

Week Seven

- What is the key element in becoming perfect and complete?
- Is there any "good" pain and suffering we have been avoiding?

*Count it all for **joy**, it states in James*
When facing trials, or when character is defamed
Possessing continuous delight is a validation
That our faith in Jesus is not an abrogation

I'm not referring to a circumstance
Where happiness exists, albeit by chance
When James says "brothers and sisters," he means those in Christ
Those who realize the depth of Jesus' sacrifice

When faith is tested, one's endurance grows
Then we experience the charm of thy repose
*Our **joy** not swayed by circumstance*
Inner delight not left to the world by chance

We must remember, we are in a fight
With powers of the dark world, the rulers of the night
We must be strong, for Satan cannot destroy
*The steadfast faith of those who "count it all for **joy**"*

Monday:

____

____

____

Tuesday: *J*oy - James 1:2

Wednesday: *O*bey - 1 Samuel 15:22

Thursday: *Y*eshua - Isaiah 7:14

Friday: What does it mean to be perfect and complete, lacking in nothing?

Saturday: Read James 1. How can we apply this to our lives?

Week Eight

- Write out all the ways God has tangibly shown His love for you. How does this make you feel?
- How are you doing when it comes to loving God as a response to His love for you? What does your love for others reveal?

__Love__ your neighbor and __love__ God, a simple command
But we struggle with this like walking through quicksand
It cannot be accomplished through our own exertion
Not achieved through humanly acts of assertion

__Love__ must become our natural response
To the Holy Spirit, our thoughts we firmly ensconce
It begins with understanding the depth of God's __love__ for me
It is only then that I'll develop the vision to see

I need to strive to __love__ others as God loves me
Agape __love__ that pours down on my soul, unconditionally
As I understand God's __love__ for all of humankind
I can then __love__ my neighbor as per Jesus' design

Monday:

___

___

___

Tuesday: *L*ove - Psalm 136

Wednesday: *O*bedience - Romans 5:19

Thursday: *V*engeance - Nahum 1:2

Friday: *E*ncouragement - Philemon 1:7

Saturday: What steps can you identify that you need to take in order to reclaim your identity in Christ and loving all?

Week Nine

The Bible tells us our bodies are a temple.

- What items need to be "cleared" of our temple for Jesus' sake?
- How do we recognize that Jesus is truly King of our lives?

The people waited excitedly for the arrival of their ***King***
Laying down palms and clothing, hallelujahs they would sing
The ***King*** *would end their bondage, Roman rule would cease*
The people were disappointed when the ***King*** *only brought peace*

The ***King*** *entered the Temple and found a den of thieves*
Jesus cleared this Temple of them while rolling up His sleeves
This carpenter is a "man among men" and showed His authority
The cleansing of many human temples is a Trilogy priority

There was healing and restoration in the middle of the fray
This same healing can occur in us; the Holy Spirit will lead the way
It starts with surrender; one must depart from every throne
Give up control to Jesus; yield all to Him alone

Yes, the Holy Spirit will work and heal the temple which is within
Restoring our being, bringing peace, granting forgiveness for our sin
Allow Christ to cleanse our temple, and then you will clearly see
The ***King's*** *great authority and His love for you and me*

Monday:

____

____

____

Tuesday: *K*ind - 1 Thessalonians 5:22

Wednesday: *I*s - Philippians 4:8

Thursday: *N*othing - Psalm 23:1

Friday: *G*ethsemane - Mark 14:32

Saturday: What is in the way of total submission to our Savior, our Lord and our King?

Week Ten

My sister got pregnant when she was a sophomore in high school. Fortunately, she put the baby up for adoption. 51 years later I got to meet my niece who tracked our family down. Although my sister will not meet Jennifer until Jen goes to heaven, I get the pleasure of knowing her here on earth. Thank you, Fran, for considering adoption and not the other potential alternatives.

Sanctity of human life is the topic for today
A controversial subject in our present culture, I'd say
Do some lives have more value? When does life begin?
Questions that must be answered from your heart, from within

At what point does someone, become a human being?
Is it size or development? To some there's no agreeing
I say there's life at conception, although I'm no great debater
Because we have been made in the likeness of our God, our Creator

I think about my tattered sweater that is in the bottom drawer
Missing buttons and discolored, it doesn't fit me anymore
But it has infinite value, and I'll explain the reason here
Because my Mom had knit and made it is the reason it's so dear

Similarly, our God has made us, He knit us in our mother's **womb**
He gave His only Son for us, we are God's precious heirloom
Life and death are the Lord's decision; of that I have no doubts
Yes, there is life and value at conception. Let the world hear my shouts

Monday:

____

____

____

Tuesday: *W*oman - Proverbs 31:30

Wednesday: *O*vercome - Romans 12:21

Thursday: *M*arriage - Genesis 2:24

Friday: *B*efore - Psalm 139:4

Saturday: Pray about when life starts. What is God saying to you?

Week Eleven

This poem, written in the Easter season, challenges our ability to keep that Spirit-filled momentum throughout the entire year. I pray we all are changed for Christ and can literally "let our light shine."

*Christ is **risen**, He is **risen** indeed*
This is an often heard Christian, Easter creed
But does the resurrection to your body feed?
Does this mean from your sins you are freed?

I know that this wasn't your aim
To attend Easter service, then go out like a flame
If Christian is the word which describes your claim
Your life should be changed; it should not be the same

Is your behavior equal to when you first began to trust
In Christ as your Savior, when He made you from dust?
No significant change, like iron turning to rust
Then one should take action, and their life should adjust

For we are a chosen people, from a royal blood line
Whose sins are forgotten; we should be on cloud nine
Like a city on a hill, please let your light shine
Let your actions give glory to Christ's name divine

Monday:

____

____

____

Tuesday: Return - Joel 2:13

Wednesday: Increase - Romans 5:20

Thursday: Saved - Titus 3:5

Friday: Effort - Hebrews 4:11

Saturday: Name - Philippians 2:10

Week Twelve

This poem was motivated by Romans 12:1-6. We need to ask ourselves:

What is my motivational gift? How do I (or can I) use that gift most effectively for God's glory in this church body? In my home and family? In my neighborhood and among my friends?

*My motivational **gift** is one of serving*
Because my path with Christ is unswerving
I do this not out of obligation, but love
Recognizing that I am full of
The grace of which I'm undeserving

*Leadership is a God given **gift***
To Christ, our focus must shift
Make it an absolute priority
To lead with biblical authority
To ensure one does not go adrift

*To teach is a **gift** not given to all*
Except to those who acknowledge God's call
Be careful that in your speech
That there is never a spoken breach
For God's Word one should never forestall

Monday:

Tuesday: Gain - 1 Timothy 6:6

____

____

____

Wednesday: Impossible - Hebrews 6:18

____

____

____

Thursday: First - 1 John 4:19

____

____

____

Friday: Truth - 3 John 1:3-4

____

____

____

Saturday: What do I need to be careful about in the use of this gift from God?

____

____

____

Week Thirteen

Inspired by Galatians 5:22-23, there are several questions which should be asked for personal reflection:

What is your most natural response to others in times that are peaceful or difficult? Is it kindness?

__Kind__ness is the fruit we're discussing today
In the present world and culture, it has become rather passe
I have learned that gracious acts are not something "I do"
As a Christian it is my being; it pervades me through and through

__Kind__ness is the outflow of God's personal love for me
Particularly important toward those with whom I disagree
The integrity of the gospel is actually at stake
An outflow of my existence, while on this globe awake

Paul states, do nothing from ambition or personal vain conceit
Regardless of status, there is no one we can mistreat
If __kind__ness is your goal, against the enemy stand resolute
Then through genuine love for Jesus, you will certainly bear this fruit

Monday:

____

____

____

Tuesday: *K*ing - Revelation 19:16

Wednesday: "*I*" - Isaiah 45:7

Thursday: *N*icodemus - John 3:4

Friday: *D*eliver - Daniel 3:17

Saturday: Read Philippians 2:5-8. Take a moment to write out your thoughts of God's kindness towards you as it relates to this passage.

Week Fourteen

Inspired by 1 Chronicles 29:12-16 and Psalm 24:1, the primary questions we need to reflect on are:

How would things be different if I lived like a manager rather than the owner? "God, what would You like me to do with Your stuff?"

One change we should make as we become an adult
Is to understand our decisions ultimately produce a result
So if we desire to live differently, our mind we must affect
Be intentional regarding the outcomes; this we should not neglect

The big truth about money, God ***owns*** *it all*
Told by the words of King David and the Apostle Paul
I am not an ***owner****; I just manage what God gives me to possess*
This is a concept I struggle with; to this I must confess

But I will ask God to transform me by the renewing of my mind
Development of great love, intimacy of the closest kind
Once this change in me has happened, I will fully realize God's goals
And allocate more resources towards the saving of lost souls

This all begins slowly; it will start with a small stride
Of giving up on worldly culture, and swallowing my pride
Then my life will change and I'll begin to more fulfill my role
Of bringing glory to my Savior, which is the ultimate goal

Monday:

____

____

____

Tuesday: *O*ffer - Romans 12:1

Wednesday: *W*alk - Isaiah 2:3

Thursday: *N*eed - 1 John 3:17

Friday: What does it mean to live like a manager rather than an owner?

Saturday: What is it in your life that you need to "disown"?

Week Fifteen

I have not pursued God my entire life and often wonder what would be if I had. Bottom line: Trust God. Trust His perfect Word and His perfect will for us and His perfect timing. I hope this can lift your day in some fashion.

Are you content with God's will for your life?
Regarding your status, your vocation, your wife?
Are you void of happiness and perhaps a debtor
Is Satan whispering softly, "You know you can do better"

Is God calling you to truth, or to live out a command?
To love your neighbor, or take an unpopular stand?
You may be waiting on God's perfect provisions
Or maybe direction to make critical decisions

If so, trust His perfect way and perfect timing
Meditate on the Word, sometimes even while rhyming
Consistently study and apply biblical truth
I have been cleansed, no more regrets of my youth

*This allows one to live **free**, no longer a slave*
Because I believe in Him Who has conquered the grave
The gospel assures us God saves by grace through faith
We can believe His promises because our great God saith

Monday:

___

___

___

Tuesday: Faith - 2 Thessalonians 1:3

Wednesday: Riches - Proverbs 11:28

Thursday: Ease - Proverbs 1:33

Friday: Effort - Hebrews 4:11

Saturday: What issue in life has you in bondage? Give it to the Lord in prayer and free yourself.

Week Sixteen

Matthew 13:44 and Matthew 6:19-21 are inspirations for this poem.

Randy Alcorn makes a reference regarding living for the "line" (eternity) and not the "dot" (our short life on this earth). This is great advice. Don't diversify when it comes to your investment in heaven.

Live not for the dot; live for the ***line***
Always ensuring your actions align
With our Savior Who has proposed the ultimate deal
Your eternal destiny secured, a fate Satan cannot steal

One has to decide: where is your true home
Do you have a plan, or do you float like styrofoam?
Are you investing in your life for eternity?
Or joining today's culture, the world's fraternity?

When one lives for the ***line*** *and not for the dot*
Finding satisfaction that has been forever sought
Living an invested life as Jesus plainly taught
At the foot of the cross, your life has been bought

The best Kingdom investment advice you will ever receive
Is "DON'T DIVERSIFY" - contrary to what the world perceives
Love the Lord with all your soul, all yourself, all your mind
An investment with infinite return, it is truly one of a kind

Monday:

____

____

____

Tuesday: Love - 1 John 4:11

Wednesday: Idle - Ecclesiastes 10:18

Thursday: Need - Hebrews 4:16

Friday: Eat - 1 Corinthians 11:27

Saturday: What are the greatest investments in your life?

Week Seventeen

While the first couple stanzas of this poem somewhat line up with the song Amazing Grace, the ending is what I would like to emphasize. It is truly Amazing Grace that our sins are erased. We need to put our faith and trust in Jesus Christ.

*Amazing **Grace** we don't deserve*
It comes from God, that's true
***Grace** is not earned and never gained*
On what we say or do

God saves us from our narcissistic being
He replaces self with love
Leading to bliss and eternity
Spent with Him in heaven above

The only question left to ask
Is whether you will embrace
The fact God cares so much for you
His Son died in your place

Yes, His Son died in your place
Your sins He will erase
Sins gone without a trace
*That is why it is Amazing **Grace***

Monday:

____

____

____

Tuesday: God - John 3:16

Wednesday: Receive - 1 Timothy 1:16

Thursday: Abraham - Galatians 3:18

Friday: Changed - 1 Corinthians 15:51

Saturday: Effect - Hebrews 9:18

Week Eighteen

People of integrity are worth imitating. I have personally done this often. The challenge is to live a life of integrity in both our public and private life. Be countercultural in today's world. Just "**Do It**."

If imitation is the sincerest form of flattery
I suggest we emulate the life of He
Who shed His blood for our sins at Calvary
I'm speaking of Jesus, the Man from Galilee

Live with integrity during our private time
Maybe even working on verse or rhyme
Living as a Christian cannot be part time
Sins of omission, my personal, greatest crime

Take action "right now" to right a wrong
Swim against culture's swift current; don't play along
Your life should show it's to Christ you belong
Gentleness and forgiveness show that you're, in fact, strong

So live a life people see and will imitate
Submit to Him, and He will make your path straight
"Live like Christ," a phrase upon which we will fixate
Integrity in our lives, we will then surely create

Monday:

Tuesday: Deliverer - Romans 11:26

Wednesday: Obey - Deuteronomy 5:27

Thursday: What is God urging you to take action on today, right now?

Friday: Integrity - 2 Corinthians 1:12

Saturday: Take - 1 Timothy 6:12

Week Nineteen

Inspired by Colossians 3:1, we need to make God's NAME great again. Look to God for solutions, not our political leaders. As God's people, are we living with divided hearts, or are we in communion and intimacy with God? This is the answer we need to confront in our minds.

Give us our leader to make America great
Yes, the US political season is one of venom and hate
Of all our candidates, their character doesn't suffice
Focus on things above, for we are raised up in Christ

The similarities are clear; we are like Israel of old
Seeking our own solutions, ignoring prophecy foretold
Continuing to ignore the Lord's obvious direction
*Refusing to **pray** for the Lord's perfect protection*

"Our country will prosper if we just elect
My candidate, whose platform is directionally correct"
Instead, we need to step back and start to reflect
On the Creator of the universe, Yahweh, the Architect

Do we trust in Christ when our world spins out of control?
Are we relying on His goodness, His virtues we always extol?
The answer is clear; we echo it with one accord
As for me and my household, we will serve the Lord

Monday:

Tuesday: Please - Galatians 6:8

____

____

____

Wednesday: Rise - John 5:29

____

____

____

Thursday: Aroma - 2 Corinthians 2:14

____

____

____

Friday: Yeast - 1 Corinthians 5:6

____

____

____

Saturday: What is your 1st response? Is it prayer or faith in the world?

____

____

____

Week Twenty

Inspired by Genesis 2 and Ephesians 5, did you know that the success of marriage in a culture often dictates the success of a culture? The Bible states **one** man and **one** woman. Please pray for our country, which has redefined marriage in a very unbiblical way.

The devil is alive and working hard to disparage
God's beautiful creation, of a man and woman, in marriage
Our culture today has worked hard to redefine
The Genesis 2 description of God's great design

Men and women are complementary; it is a biological fact
Children need a mother and father, and both shall interact
To ensure the wellbeing of the children they raise
Marriage commits both parents to the end of their days

In recent years, marriage has been weakened by a revisionist view
Brought about by adult desires, seeking to undo
The anthropological, biological, and God ordained truth
Delinking childbearing from marriage, scarring our youth

I earnestly pray our country and world leaders recognize
That the redefinition of marriage will seriously compromise
The fibers of society's fabric in which we exist
God's definition of marriage cannot be dismissed

Monday:

____

____

____

Tuesday: Obvious - Galatians 5:19

Wednesday: Naked - Genesis 2:25

Thursday: Eden - Ezekiel 28:13

Friday: Read Ephesians 5. How do we follow God's example in verse 1?

Saturday: In Ephesians 5:15, the Bible states, "Be very careful, then, how you live." What does this mean?

Week Twenty-One

Inspired by John 14:27, how do we achieve true peace in our workplace, our homes, our church, and our world without risking our integrity? One way that has helped me immensely is to become "a professional forgiver."

Give your burdens to the Lord, and He will take care of you
Sounds easy, but Lord, You know what I've been through
I must take action and address all of this strife
I must personally deal with the stresses in my life

Now that I've tried to solve all my problems on my own
I've found the solution, all along I should have known
*To make **peace** with the world gives no permanent relief*
It simply adds to the delight of the ultimate thief

*If true **peace** or Shalom is what you're looking for*
Like a drink offering, to Christ, your life should pour
Love God and love your neighbor, should be the goal
*Only this brings reconciliation and **peace** to your soul*

There is a yoke that is easy and a burden which is light
A lamp for your feet and a path which is right
It comes from intimacy with our Good Creator
*And it shall open the door to a **peace** much greater*

Monday:

____

____

____

Tuesday: Profound - Psalm 92:5

Wednesday: Eat - 1 Corinthians 10:31

Thursday: Alert - 1 Peter 4:7

Friday: Calm - Proverbs 29:11

Saturday: Effort - 2 Peter 1:5

Week Twenty-Two

This poem focusing on the fruit of the Spirit attribute of patience was inspired by a sermon, which highlighted the song "Nobody Wants To Die" by John Fischer. I suggest you search for it on YouTube. The lyrics are enlightening, and the 3rd stanza of this poem is from John Fischer's song.

The definition of patience, I need to reacquaint
It is "to endure discomfort without complaint"
A trait rarely seen anymore within the masses
Even when I'm looking through my rose colored glasses

We want the results without knowing the "whys"
Shunning the time, energy, and pain, of multiple tries
*Immediate solutions, we want everything "**NOW**"*
Or to this task, we will quickly disavow

We want to be a winner without taking a loss
We want to be a disciple without counting the cost
We want to follow Jesus, but the cross we just walk by
Everyone wants to get to heaven, Lord, but nobody wants to die

There is a process which will develop this fruit
The first step is a decision we must faithfully execute
Intimacy with Jesus, our first and foremost pursuit
Then through this journey, one can be resolute

Monday:

____

____

____

Tuesday: *N*eighbor - Exodus 20:17

____

____

____

Wednesday: *O*vercome - Matthew 16:18

____

____

____

Thursday: *W*orld - Mark 16:15

____

____

____

Friday: What are the causes of an impatient society?

____

____

____

Saturday: Do you have any possessions or habits which contribute to your impatience?

____

____

____

Week Twenty-Three

This is based upon the Fruit of the Spirit verses in Galatians 5:22–23 speaking to the "strength of gentleness." Is this possible? Yet our great Creator is the most powerful, yet the most gentle Being in the universe. NOT an oxymoron.

The "strength of gentleness," an oxymoron?
I can't imagine how this can be
Any person stating this must be trying to con
Their audience into a fantasy

One sees our culture and our world
As dog-eat-dog, let's climb our way to the top
Our work is primary, family life is unfurled
Our ego doesn't know how to stop

But we should pause, fill our lungs with air
Humbly submit to His divine will
Reflect on His kindness, grace and care
Take His yoke, find rest and be ***still***

For God is completely gentle with me
He has forgiven me for all of my sin
And because of this endless mercy
I will show gentleness to all from within

Monday:

____

____

____

Tuesday: Still - Psalm 46:10

Wednesday: Trust - Psalm 56:3

Thursday: Idenity - Galatians 3:26

Friday: Loss - 2 Corinthians 1:4

Saturday: Love - 2 John 1:6

Week Twenty-Four

Our culture (and our politics) have redefined marriage recently. We need to examine what is marriage according to God. Marriage is intended to reflect God's glory (Ephesians 5:22-32) and Malachi 2:14. These verses illustrate marriage is a covenant, not a contract. Reflect on the difference between a covenant and a contract.

Marriage is God's doing, yes it is His design
That a man and woman enter a covenant so divine
A covenant we seal with a solemn vow
A gift our culture has distorted in the here and now

Culture would have us believe it matters not your gender
As long as the person is loving, gentle, and tender
Some say marriage is not permanent; it's just a phase of our life
I can always find a new partner, husband or ***wife***

But alas, the Bible clearly states that this cannot be
Marriage is not a pledge of two, but in fact a covenant of three
Only God can enable two fleshes to truly become one
A consecrated union, never to come undone

My personal relationship with Christ is the key ingredient
To Kim and my firm marriage foundation, yes, this is being obedient
One primary thought which I will add additionally
It is only God Who enables husband and ***wife*** *to love unconditionally*

Monday:

___

___

___

Tuesday: *W*ait - Lamentations 3:26

Wednesday: *I*s - Proverbs 31:30

Thursday: *F*ar More - Proverbs 31:10

Friday: *E*verything - Ephesians 5:24

Saturday: What does the word "covenant" mean to you?

Week Twenty-Five

Based upon Luke 10:25-37, where we wrestle with the question and the challenge of truly needing to understand who our neighbor is. Is it proximity, relationship, affinity? What defines your neighbor? I would submit anyone we encounter is truly our neighbor.

The 10th Chapter of Luke will lead my thoughts today
With hope that this touches your life in some way
It begins where Jesus sends out the seventy-two
Because the harvest is great, but workers are few

Then Jesus tells of a man travelling to Jericho
Robbed and beaten by bandits, no hope for tomorrow
The moral of the story is to focus your labor
Not upon yourself, but in loving your neighbor

*"**Who** is my neighbor?" is the question that was raised*
From an expert of law, expecting to be praised
The expert's own mouth, replied "the neighbor shows kindness"
In contrast to those who walked by, their hearts hardened with blindness

Luke's words are well written; the mandate is clear
To heed not this message is to be very cavalier
To be a good worker and neighbor should be our goal
With our names inscribed clearly on God's holy scroll

Monday:

____

____

____

Tuesday: *W*ho - Luke 10:29

Wednesday: *H*ave Taken - Psalm 88:18

Thursday: *O*ur - Romans 15:2

Friday: Read Luke Chapter 10.

Saturday: Who is someone in your life you need to treat as a neighbor?

Week Twenty-Six

We honor God by honoring the relationships He has placed us in and the roles He has given us. We honor Christ by allowing His love to flow through us in our relationships and when our lives are a reflection of Who He is.

*In our relationships, are we **honoring** the Lord?*
Are we Spirit filled, is it love we are pointed toward?
*Do we **honor** Christ as we live our daily life?*
Husbands, look in the mirror; are you truly loving your wife?

Because a husband's role for his family is to lead
His wife will dutifully help is what Genesis 2 decreed
The husband's love should earn his wife's total respect
A godly marriage is an easy marriage to protect

Children, scripture says, your parents you must obey
*Treat them with **honor**, do not create an affray*
For if you follow this very simple command
Your years will be long, and your life will be grand

And as you earn your wages, toil for God and not for men
Ensure all at work see Christ in you, time and time again
For if we do all the above, our lives are a reflection of Who Christ is
And this will surely show the world our lives are truly His

Monday:

___

___

___

Tuesday: Holy - 1 Peter 1:16

Wednesday: Our - Genesis 19:32

Thursday: Noah - Genesis 6:8

Friday: Our - Matthew 6:9

Saturday: Right - Psalm 23:3

Week Twenty-Seven

This ode is based upon Ephesians 6:10-20. After reflecting on this, we need to ask the question:

Are there any specific areas of your personal life that the Holy Spirit has been revealing to you where sin remains and you have given the devil a foothold?

Put on the armor of God, a very direct verse
On the surface, it seems very clear
You're a warrior, be strong, to Satan be perverse
Then through the battle, one can persevere

But I would say there's more to this text
And it points to acknowledging our own weakness
For the battle is spiritual; there's no pretext
And will be won through humbleness and meekness

For this conflict is against dark spiritual powers
Which require God's supernatural strength
Are you willing to put in the prayerful hours?
Or will you not wrestle, but tarry at arm's length?

So put on the armor, prepare for the fight
Against the devil, we will stand ***firm***
Pray in the Spirit; use all of His might
Our faith and love in Christ we will affirm

Monday:

___

___

___

Tuesday: Foundation - 1 Timothy 6:19

Wednesday: If - Isaiah 7:9

Thursday: Resist - 1 Peter 5:9

Friday: Mighty - Job 36:5

Saturday: What steps do you need to / can you take to be more alert in the battle for your soul?

Week Twenty-Eight

This poem is based upon 1 Thessalonians 2:17-20 given by a guest pastor. His email address has the suffix: "lovegodlovepeopleproveit". This basically summarizes the point of this ode. Contrast the Galatians verses with those in Isaiah 14.

*How **I** live my life matters*
A subject of great meaning
***I** have tasted the spiritual milk*
Now it's time to start the weaning

***I** will run to win the prize*
*Yes in Christ **I** will immerse*
***I** will strive for my reward*
To this world I'll become adverse

It is time to live for others
*From the world's lifeboat **I** will swim*
Focusing on Christ and not this culture
Total dependence upon Him

***I** am all in; **I** will be diligent*
It is Jesus I'm pointed toward
***I** will suffer for doing what's right*
*So **I** may receive my full reward*

Monday:

____

____

____

Tuesday: *"I"* - Isaiah 14:13-14

Wednesday: What "I" statements are in my life?

Thursday: Read: Galatians 1:6. How fast do we depart from the gospel?

Friday: Read Galatians 1:10

Saturday: Whose approval are we trying to win?

Week Twenty-Nine

Here, we are reading and writing about James 3:13-18 and considering true wisdom. What steps can we take to grow in wisdom?

- Ask for it with no doubting and in humbleness
- Surround yourself with wise people
- Find a mentor

Whose wisdom are you living by?
Is the sermon for today
The wisdom seen by culture's eye
Or walking in the Lord's way?

This topic is writ in great detail
By James in Chapter Three
Words I pray can be of great avail
In how they apply to me

"I have wisdom," I've often said
Commonly with tongue in cheek
I must become what most dread
To gain wisdom I must become weak

Yes pureness, mercy, and a mild heart
Are the cornerstone of James' story
True wisdom can only truly start
*When one gives God **<u>all</u>** the glory*

Monday:

____

____

____

Tuesday: *A*sk - James 1:5

Wednesday: *L*ord - Psalm 111:10

Thursday: *L*ives - Proverbs 11:30

Friday: Read James 3:13-18. How does real wisdom reveal itself in our actions?

Saturday: Read James 3:17 again. How are these characteristics showing up in your life?

Week Thirty

From James chapter 3, we need to examine whether our tongue is an indicator of good character or bad character. A defiled tongue will stain the whole person. Read Psalm 141:3 to also help frame this poem.

A lesson we should learn, whether old or young
Is that an indicator of character comes from the tongue
Jesus states we will be judged by what we say
We should not allow our language to slip into decay

A transformed mind produces a transformed life
Thoughtless ***words****, however, can cut like a knife*
Our speech can encourage and endorse
Or cause destruction while often being very coarse

A defiled tongue can also permanently stain
When intentionally harsh or used to feign
So please take control of what I say, O Lord
Let my ***words*** *sound like a well played chord*

Let my speech reflect prayer and also praise
Let it witness to others and also raise
All glory to You, Lord, is what I declare
This is my desire and also my personal prayer

Monday:

____

____

____

Tuesday: Wordless - Romans 8:26

Wednesday: Of God - Hebrews 4:12

Thursday: Rather - 1 Corinthians 14:19

Friday: Distort - 2 Corinthians 4:2

Saturday: Spirit - 1 Corinthians 2:13

Week Thirty-One

Rooted in James 2, this poem examines our heart condition. This also asks the questions: What are the sins that you struggle with that you have made acceptable as a follower of Christ? In what ways do these stunt your growth in Christ?

Satan, the ultimate thief
Enjoys planting the belief
*That intellectual **faith** in the mind*
Will be the saving grace of mankind

Now knowledge of God is terrific
But James is very specific
He will not allow you to be misled
*James states: "**Faith** without works is dead"*

***Faith** and works cannot be apart*
For the Christian who has a right heart
Will do deeds which bear much fruit
To Christ they are absolute

This ode's purpose is not remorse
But to slightly alter the course
And assist in playing a small part
For the Holy Spirit to soften our heart

Monday:

Tuesday: Fulfill - 2 Chronicles 36:22

Wednesday: Acknowledge - John 12:42

Thursday: Increase - Luke 17:5

Friday: True - Acts 14:22, Titus 1:4

Saturday: Hearing - Romans 10:17

Week Thirty-Two

Brokenness is not an adjective our culture readily accepts. However, Jesus' paradox of brokenness is a call to be different. In God's economy, brokenness gives birth to new life as a Christian.

What exactly does "poor in spirit" mean?
To be unwealthy, sad, or perhaps unclean?
The Greek word ptochos is used, and it conveys
A complete lack of resources all your days

Then Jesus uses the word "pentheo" for those who mourn
This is deep inner agony, feeling like an infinite scorn
We mourn over our sin before our mother gives birth
We mourn for God to come back and restore this ***<u>broken</u>*** *earth*

So in what way, exactly, have the ***<u>broken</u>*** *been blessed?*
Another paradox from our Creator as you may have guessed
The ***<u>broken</u>*** *have given up this world for one of eternity*
Where they will be restored and comforted so perfectly

In God's economy, ***<u>brokenness</u>*** *gives birth to new living*
Giving up my worldly desires to a Maker so forgiving
Exhibiting love for man and a humble meekness
For God to exhibit His power is made perfect in weakness

Monday:

____

____

____

Tuesday: Brokenhearted - Psalm 34:18

Wednesday: Rope (cord) - Ecclesiastes 4:12

Thursday: Oppresses - Ezekiel 18:12

Friday: Kind - Proverbs 19:17

Saturday: Escaped - Psalm 124:7

Week Thirty-Three

Please read Romans 11:33-36 for the roots of this poem. God alone is worthy of our praise. Only He deserves the glory. Hallelujah!

*To God alone be the **glory***
That is surely the only true story
I provide rhyme to a phrase
But I'm not looking for your praise

*To God alone be the **glory***
All laud to Him be mandatory
A wise and true, desirable confession
To be like Him, my true obsession

*To God alone be the **glory***
He is not some allegory
I speak with Him throughout my day
Unbelievers, grace for you, I pray

*To God alone be the **glory***
Effort less than 100% is derogatory
Praise to Him, my true endeavor
*To Him be all the **glory** forever*

Amen

Monday:

___

___

___

Tuesday: *G*od - Jude 25

Wednesday: *L*ord - Habakkuk 2:14

Thursday: *O*verjoyed - 1 Peter 4:13

Friday: *R*adiance - Hebrews 1:3

Saturday: *Y*ou - Colossians 3:4

Week Thirty-Four

Our Savior is truly merciful. Mercy, however, is not appreciated in our world. Some questions for reflection: In what ways have you found it difficult to show mercy for others? Who are people in your sphere that the Holy Spirit is revealing to you that you should show mercy to?

When Jesus walked this earth, Roman culture
*Thought **mercy** to be a disease of the soul*
Military might, strength, and power were
Always the Roman focus and the goal

*However, **mercy** is at the core of Who God is*
And Who He desires us to be
*As a Christian, displaying **mercy** in your life*
Becomes an absolute key

*One does not "do" **mercy**. No it is*
Intertwined in your being
Forgiving and compassionate is
What people should be seeing

Selflessness borne from love
Is what our lives showcase
To emulate God's love, that is:
Unconditional forgiveness, compassion, and grace

Monday:

____

____

____

Tuesday: Mercy - Hosea 6:6

Wednesday: End - Nehemiah 9:31

Thursday: Reason - 1 Timothy 1:16

Friday: Cry - Psalm 28:6

Saturday: Yahweh - 1 Chronicles 21:13

Week Thirty-Five

Based upon Romans 12:3-8, pride often is an obstacle to living a true, Christian life. I must realize to be first is to be last, and to be great is to be a slave to all (Mark 10:43-45).

I constantly struggle with my pride
Always putting myself first
In this world I would abide
Others seeing me at my worst

Realizing this is a fight
And from within there must be change
Removal from my ***body****, the spite*
God, my heart you must rearrange

True humility is to recognize
Right thinking always starts with God
Time for us to realize
It's only to Him we must applaud

For gospel living is a sword
That we must show to all we meet
To imitate Him, what we work toward
Giving and loving for a life replete

Monday:

Tuesday: *B*ody - Romans 12:4

Wednesday: *O*ne - Ephesians 4:25

Thursday: *D*one - 1 Corinthians 14:26

Friday: *Y*ou - Numbers 6:24

Saturday: How may we honor God by putting ourselves last?

Week Thirty-Six

Honoring all above ourselves is a great tenant to live by. This is true at work, at our homes, and in our community. Christians should be a very humble "**proud**."

Three qualities that all should see
When anyone looks at Christianity
Are writ in Romans 12. This is where Paul paints the scene
Very clearly and candidly ending in verse sixteen

Empathy for others is a trait
That should be visible on our breastplate
Making other's situations into our own
Rejoice with those who rejoice, moan with those who moan

This verse also states with all certainty
That we are to live in complete harmony
One is to stand for truth, but win people by our love
Prevent callous situations like a batting glove

Paul wrote that it is good for our stability
That we honor all above ourselves, and live in humility
View not through the lens of this world, but as God does see
This will allow one to enjoy all company

Monday:

____

____

____

Tuesday: Paul - Acts 22:3

____

____

____

Wednesday: Race - 2 Timothy 4:7

____

____

____

Thursday: Opposes - James 4:6

____

____

____

Friday: Under - 1 Peter 5:6

____

____

____

Saturday: Detests - Proverbs 16:5

____

____

____

Week Thirty-Seven

Blessed persecution. Is there such a thing? The Bible states emphatically "yes." Think about what reasons we have to rejoice when we are facing persecution. How does the Bible prepare us to stand in the face of persecution?

This ode will address the last beatitude
Which challenges my thoughts and my attitude
God blesses those who are persecuted for doing right
I'm not sure this is something I want to invite

While in parts of this world, faith can result in earthly demise
And faith in Christ may cause some to "euthanize"
Here in the States, our biggest challenge is compromise
Will we stand up for Jesus, or wear a disguise?

For if persecution is what you wish to avoid
There are many strategies which can be easily employed
Water down the gospel, and live like many on this globe
"Go along to get along," then no one will probe

The world wants us to cower and be ashamed
To blend in with the crowd, His Word never proclaimed
But Jesus says be ***bold*** *in our witness, yes, this is His command*
For He is our fortress, on Christ we will stand

Monday:

____

____

____

Tuesday: Blessed - Matthew 5:11

Wednesday: Opening - Ephesians 6:19

Thursday: Lion - Proverbs 28:1

Friday: Do - Psalm 56:4

Saturday: How do we pray to become bold in our faith?

Week Thirty-Eight

Romans 13:8-14 is the basis for this poem, which asks the question: What would occur if we showed love towards every individual we meet? Interesting, but difficult question.

At the risk of starting to belabor
Love does no harm to a neighbor
What if this became our daily theme?
What if this became mainstream?

Yes, we all have a continuing debt
And that is to love all that we have met
Love the Lord our God with all of our heart
Love continuously until this earth we do depart

All prejudices within we are to reject
We love all people is what our Lord does expect
Through the world's darkness, our light will shine
This culture's insults to ourselves are benign

Behave in a Christlike way to all people, all the time
Perhaps spread the Word and goodwill through a simple rhyme
Push through darkness, and clothe ourselves with the armor of light
Finish the race with faith and ***fight*** *the good* ***fight***

Monday:

____

____

____

Tuesday: Fight - Nehemiah 4:20

Wednesday: "I" - 1 Corinthians 9:26

Thursday: God - Deuteronomy 3:22

Friday: Have - 1 Timothy 4:7

Saturday: Take - 1 Timothy 6:12

Week Thirty-Nine

Based upon Romans 15:1-13, which challenges us to be accepting of all people. Love them in the truth of the gospel.

In Romans 15:7, Paul gives a command
To accept each other and not be so grand
Accept means welcome or receive, not just tolerate
A call to completely love and cast off all forms of hate

Complete acceptance in the church will build unity
Which will show God's glory in the community
Can one imagine the church without a split?
Where it is difficult to identify a hypocrite

Verse 13 is a favorite because it helps me cope
By reminding me that God is the source of all hope
Believers trust in God Whose love and power never fail
While the world continues its quest for the "holy grail"

Therefore I put my ***trust*** *in Jesus and give up all control*
For human comforts and security were never His goal
God has spoken plainly through His Word and the Spirit
My earnest simple prayer is "give me ears to hear it"

Monday:

____

____

____

Tuesday: Truth - 1 Timothy 2:4

Wednesday: Remnant - Zephaniah 3:12

Thursday: Understand - Ephesians 5:17

Friday: Secret - Proverbs 11:13

Saturday: Take - Psalm 27:14

Week Forty

Based upon John 11:1-44, John reveals several truths about brokenness. Firstly, we need God's light to guide us through our dark periods; God can help you overcome any hardship; and lastly God didn't want any hardship to ever occur to us. He created a perfect earth. We as humans chose to taint it.

In our culture, we embellish more than we should
And perhaps put on the face that all is good
But there are many in life living with countless despairs
Wondering if there is anyone who really cares

With Instagram and Twitter and "The Facebook"
Broadcasting to the world, one's active and happy outlook
Let's be aware of those whose words are unspoken
Who may be in need, and whose spirit is broken

The only way I've found to rid myself of this gloom
Is to rely on He, borne of a virgin's womb
To navigate through hardships, I need God's light as a ***guide***
His Word as my sword, His Spirit living inside

This is what gives us our joy and our hope
Not the world's view, but seeing through God's periscope
Then your spirit will thrive without a doubt
Wiping away your brokenness, hearing "Lazarus, come out"

Monday:

Tuesday: Guard - Proverbs 4:23

Wednesday: Unity - Psalm 133:1

Thursday: Ill - Proverbs 12:21

Friday: Discern - 1 Kings 3:11

Saturday: End Times - John 14:2

Week Forty-One

Psalm 22 and David's relationship with God are the model for this ode. While David wasn't perfect and sinned considerably, he was a "man after God's heart." I pray we also are pursuing God's heart with the greatest passion and laying our sin at the **cross**.

Measure your Jesus relationship, if you truly dare
A test of which is the width and depth of your prayer
Do you truly "run to win" with eyes upon the eternal prize?
Or is it superficial, fooling mortals with your guise?

Is your prayer life intimate; are you in love with your Maker, Dad?
Is the communication sporadic, maybe somewhat like a fad?
Is your prayer life focused on self or finely honed into God?
Is it brutally honest, giving Him all glory and laud

Our relationship with God is the most crucial of this life
More important than money or even choosing husband or wife
The good news is there's time, if you are presently reading this page
And it matters not your status, your color, or your age

As you increase your prayers, you won't keep God at arm's length
And you will lean upon His wisdom and draw upon His strength
Intimacy develops, and the relationship will thrive
God will change your behavior, and you will come alive

Monday:

____

____

____

Tuesday: Choose - Joshua 24:15

Wednesday: Run - 1 Corinthians 9:24

Thursday: Owe - Romans 13:7

Friday: Sharpen - Proverbs 27:17

Saturday: Serve - 1 Peter 4:10

Week Forty-Two

The fruit of the Holy Spirit is? Read Galatians 5:16-26. Reflect upon what the outflows of your life are. Do these outflows reflect the trait of a person who is walking in the Spirit, or one struggling in the works of the flesh (or a combination of both)?

In today's culture, we must be keenly aware
Not to lose our identity in Christ, and not to compare
Our lives to one another or become so works driven
We ignore God's great gift of the Holy Spirit we've been given

Our own efforts are futile and mostly end in failure
Until we accept the Holy Spirit, sent by our Savior
It is written in the Bible, these words we can't refute
The Holy Spirit in your life will only produce good fruit

We must all make a decision; will we live in our own viewpoint?
Caught up in our possessions, our culture we will not disappoint
*Or throw away the **flesh** and make the Spirit your choice*
Develop intimacy with God, and listen to His inner voice

Consider your struggles to walk with the Spirit; identify the reasons
Recognize that your life may need a major change of season
Align yourself with God's Word, along with the admission
That we can only claim His throne by the act of total submission

Monday:

Tuesday: *F*aith - Galatians 5:6

Wednesday: *L*ove - 1 Corinthians 13:13

Thursday: *E*ffort - Romans 9:16

Friday: *S*truggle - Philippians 1:30

Saturday: *H*oly - Leviticus 19:2, 1 Peter 1:16

Week Forty-Three

Think about the things a crucified Savior saves us from:

The guilt of sin – Hebrews 10:5-14
The wrath of God – Romans 1:18-19
A guilty conscience – Hebrews 10:22
The fear of death – Hebrews 2:11-15
Satan's power – Colossians 1:13-14

For our salvation, we need a crucified Savior
Let's learn of Jesus, starting with His behavior
Although He is God, Christ came down to earth
Lived a sinless life, starting right from birth

Jesus is the Paschal Lamb; He died on the cross
Gave His life so my life would not end in loss
Christ saves me from the guilt of sin, God's holy wrath
The curse of the law, and Satan's deceitful path

Jesus brings forgiveness of sins; God remembers them no more
The cross is the perfect sacrifice; your life is ***paid*** *for*
We receive God's love and favor; with the Holy Spirit
Available for all who accept God's Word when they hear it

The Lamb looked like it died, but now is centered on the throne
And will come again to rule, although the time is unknown
My prayer for us all, now that this ode's coming to an end
Is for intimacy with Jesus, in only Him we will depend

Monday:

Tuesday: Philip - Acts 8:6

____

____

____

Wednesday: Approach - Hebrews 4:16

____

____

____

Thursday: In - Psalm 4:5

____

____

____

Friday: Died - 2 Corinthians 5:14

____

____

____

Saturday: Have you or someone you know not accepted Christ's free gift to each and every one of us?

____

____

____

Week Forty-Four

Celebrating my wife's and my adult baptism (it occurred the same day) and making a public profession of our faith.

Strengthening my walk with God
On the day after November 28th
Being obedient to my Master
Publically declaring my faith

*Being submerged in the **water***
And in my heart displace
The desires of this world with the
Peace, Love, and Joy of God's grace

Accepting the forgiveness
Of the One who created me
Our God, Whose perfect patience
Has always awaited me

*This **water** which gives me*
Spiritual awakening and rebirth
And a love so encompassing it
Can save all on this earth

Monday:

____

____

____

Tuesday: Walk - 1 John 1:7

Wednesday: All - Exodus 7:20

Thursday: Thirsty - Revelation 21:6

Friday: Earth - Isaiah 55:10

Saturday: Rivers - John 7:38

Week Forty-Five

*I will **deny** three times*
That I even knew my Lord
Yes, I've committed these crimes
His love I have ignored

Can I count during the day
When I shun His absolute truth
Little lies, neglecting to pray
It's clear when you act as a sleuth

But I didn't hold the spike
Being driven through His wrist
With the whip I didn't strike
I didn't betray Christ with a kiss

No, my betrayal is not so loud
It's like a gentle unnoticed tide
Yes, it blends into the crowd
Subtleness being my bride

If my worship has become
Just motions with no intent
My spiritual life gone numb
No real intention to repent

Time to get down on my knees
And recognize God's grace
It's moments just like these
That restore me to that place

Of knowing that He forgives
All sinners just like me
Yes, the Lord forever lives
My forgiveness granted on that tree

Monday:

Tuesday: *D*ecide - Joshua 24:15

Wednesday: *E*ducate - Proverbs 3:6

Thursday: *N*ervous - Philippians 4:6

Friday: *Y*oke - Matthew 11:28-29

Saturday: How am I denying the Lord?

Week Forty-Six

Am I ready to see King Jesus? If not, why not? What should I do?
If I am ready to see King Jesus, how do I help others prepare?

We live in the US, and there are problems in our nation
But that should not deter us from living with eager anticipation
Of our Lord Jesus Christ to be revealed
Only He has the solution, then our world will be healed

We should strive to live in constant dependence
On the One Who willingly endured the ultimate sentence
All glory to Him, our actions should be resolute
Always aspiring in our life to produce good fruit

Faithful stewardship is integral in waiting for the King
For in heaven this generosity causes angels to sing
Love of money has caused many to wander in their faith
One cannot love both God and mammon, Matthew's gospel sayeth

Our love for our King has a key ingredient
Which is that this love causes us to be completely ***obedient***
If you understand anything from this simple rhyme
It is to live ready; be vigilant, all the time

Monday:

____

____

____

Tuesday: Offer - 1 Peter 4:9

Wednesday: Bible (Book of the Law) - Joshua 1:8

Thursday: Establish - Proverbs 16:3

Friday: Yield - Proverbs 3:14

Saturday: What steps can I take to become a better watchman?

Week Forty-Seven

As Christians, we recognize that holiness cannot be achieved on our own by following a set of rules.

We are made by God, for God, and live for His glory
But that is not all there is to this story
One must get ready to die, yes, your life you will lose
The Holy Spirit into your heart will transfuse

Without the Spirit, our efforts are truly for naught
We accomplish nothing; our actions are fraught
If upon Christ we truly wish to build
Then with the Holy Spirit we also must be filled

So I'll develop a plan with the ultimate goal
Of allowing the Spirit to take complete control
So how do I accomplish this? What's the design?
I desire a strategy, a very clear guideline

First, die to ***self****, and make a prayerful request*
Become intimate with Christ, and expect to be blessed
Keep away from anything that takes God's place in your heart
Then the Spirit will fill you and make you His work of art

Monday:

Tuesday: *S*erve - 1 Peter 4:10

Wednesday: *E*mpower - 2 Corinthians 12:9

Thursday: *L*ift - 1 Peter 5:6

Friday: *F*ocus - Colossians 3:2

Saturday: In what areas of my life do I need to die to myself?

Week Forty-Eight

Matthew 1 and 2 gives the direction for this poem and leads us to the following conclusions:

- Hope in this world ALWAYS fails.
- Hope placed in Jesus NEVER fails.
- The choice is in where we place our hope.

What do our thoughts and lives reveal
*About what we place our **hope** in?*
Concern about where one gets their next meal
Or in the stock market will we win?

When we place our trust in this world
We will undoubtedly fail
Watching our lives come completely unfurled
Our future is very frail

But faith in Jesus comes with a vow
That God will always keep
He's with us in the here and now
His promises He will keep

So regardless of our time on earth
Whether very long or very brief
God's love is with us from before our birth
*Faith, **Hope,** and Love will quench our grief*

Monday:

____

____

____

Tuesday: *H*arvest - Luke 10:2

Wednesday: *O*vercome - 1 John 5:4

Thursday: *P*artner - Philemon 1:17

Friday: *E*very - 2 Corinthians 10:5

Saturday: Where in our lives do we need to improve our choices?

Week Forty-Nine

Please read Matthew 5:5. Jesus changes our understanding of meek. In addition, Jesus' words were a direct rebuke against the religious climate of the day. Please contemplate how pride is destructive and how Jesus reveals that a truly blessed life is lived with an eternal perspective.

At the lowest point of this tired, gray world
Out of thought, all emotions unfurled
Feeling the weight of a huge landslide
This culture leaves me empty and unsatisfied

This orb promises riches, but left me broke
Until I learned, from this world I must unyoke
I recognize my sin and spiritual impoverishment
But then found the answer, to my astonishment

To achieve fulfillment, I must dive headfirst
To the One Who quenches all hunger and thirst
God's righteousness is where my strength is found
Only here from bondage can I become unbound

Only God can satisfy and ensure you are filled
Hunger and thirst for Him, and He will build
You into a courageous soul who is infinitely blessed
Who has lightened your yoke and found you ***rest***

Monday:

___

___

___

Tuesday: Race - 2 Timothy 4:7

Wednesday: Everything - Hebrews 12:1

Thursday: Strength - Isaiah 40:29

Friday: Testimony - John 19:35

Saturday: Read Matthew 11:28-29. How can we apply these verses?

Week Fifty

Based upon Romans 12:1-2, this poem focuses on what rules your mind. Please consider your thoughts.

Yes it is true, that I was blind
Until transformed by the renewal of my ***mind***
I once was sightless, but now I see
How God is molding me to all I can be

Myself I offer, a living sacrifice
To the One Who has paid the ultimate price
Yes, He was rich, yet for me became poor
So that I could enter through salvation's door

Sin gone away, it's no longer my boss
Washed by His blood and His death on the cross
I now live for Christ, a life set apart
Continually striving for the softening of my heart

Humbled I kneel, covered in His grace
Understanding He has created this world and all space
Conform I will not, transformed I will fulfill
To live in His good, pleasing and perfect will

Monday:

Tuesday: *M*outh - Romans 10:10

Wednesday: *I*dentity - Psalm 139:14

Thursday: *N*ew - 2 Corinthians 5:17

Friday: *D*ust - Psalm 113:7

Saturday: Are there any areas of our mind that need renewal?

Week Fifty-One

A poem which challenges how I love. Hate all sin within myself. Romans 12:9 which reads: "Love must be sincere. Hate what is evil; cling to what is good." Great words to live by.

Love must be sincere
Our Lord has made that very clear
We love with no hypocrisy
A love visible for all to see

We must also hate all that is evil
Yes, from our lives, stage a great upheaval
Genuine love cannot love everything
But sheds the vile and applauds the pleasing

*We are also to **cling** to all that is good*
Undivided devotion is what we should
Be showing to all that we humbly serve
Of His endless grace that we do not deserve

Yes, Jesus died for His enemy's sakes; we should do the same
Refusing all contrary to His will should be our greatest aim
We can do all this through Him Who gives us strength
But intimacy with Christ is the key; it will not happen at arm's length

Monday:

Tuesday: Confidence - 2 Corinthians 7:16

Wednesday: Leave - Hebrews 13:5

Thursday: Integrity - Proverbs 10:9

Friday: Nothing - Philippians 2:3

Saturday: Gratitude - Acts 24:3

Week Fifty-Two

Selfish prayers, lack of concern for the lost. I intentionally ended this book with this poem. I pray the words in this book will help you with your relationship with Jesus, our Savior, and convict us to rapidly spread the Word to those who do not know of His saving grace.

My heart is heavy, my eyes should weep
For all people who are spiritually asleep
Concern I should feel and in the same fashion
Praying for the lost should be my personal passion

Like a speeding bullet from a hot firearm
I hope these words, Lord, can sound an internal alarm
But I speak with you, Lord, and when I pray
I hear mostly requests that I get "my" own way

*It is time for me to **wake**, for You're coming soon*
Whether decades from now or before the next moon
I want to be prepared and in the camp
Of meeting the Bridegroom, with oil in my lamp

Wasting time is a habit I must surely quit
Because now is the time to fully commit
My chips all in, living a life fervent
To hear, "Well done, my good and faithful servant."

Monday:

___

___

___

Tuesday: Wisdom - Proverbs 8:11

Wednesday: Awake - Psalm 57:8

Thursday: Kindness - Colossians 3:12, Galatians 5:22

Friday: Endurance - Colossians 1:11

Saturday: Have you given your life to Christ? This is the most important decision you will ever make.

Yes or No?

ABC's of Faith

ADMIT THAT YOU'RE A SINNER. This is where that godly sorrow leads to genuine repentance for sinning against the righteous God and there is a genuine, observable change of heart, where God changes our hearts and regenerates us from the inside out.

Romans 3:10 - As it is written: "There is no one righteous, not even one;

Romans 3:23 - for all have sinned and fall short of the glory of God,

Romans 6:23 - For the wages of sin is death, but the gift of God is eternal life in Christ Jesus our Lord.

BELIEVE IN YOUR HEART THAT JESUS CHRIST DIED FOR YOUR SINS, WAS BURIED, AND THAT GOD RAISED JESUS FROM THE DEAD. This is trusting with 100% of your being that Jesus Christ is Who He said He was.

Romans 10:9-10 - 9 If you declare with your mouth, "Jesus is Lord," and believe in your heart that God raised him from the dead, you will be saved. 10 For it is with your heart that you believe and are justified, and it is with your mouth that you profess your faith and are saved.

CALL UPON THE NAME OF THE LORD. **Every single person who ever lived will bend their knee and that Jesus Christ is Lord, the Lord of Lords and the King of Kings.**

Romans 10:9-10 - [9] If you declare with your mouth, "Jesus is Lord," and believe in your heart that God raised him from the dead, you will be saved. [10] For it is with your heart that you believe and are justified, and it is with your mouth that you profess your faith and are saved.

Romans 10:13 - for, "Everyone who calls on the name of the Lord will be saved

We must carefully consider the cost of following Jesus. While grace is free, there is a great cost and significance in following Jesus.

Made in the USA
Middletown, DE
05 December 2023

44673751R00066